PIANO · VOCAL · GUITAR

THE BEST EASY LISTENING SONGS EVER

Hal Leonard Publishing Corporation

7777 West Bluemound Road P.O. Box 13819 Milwaukee, WI 53213

ISBN 0-7935-0867-3

ALL OUT OF LOVE

Words and Music by GRAHAM RUSSELL
and CLIVE DAVIS

I'm ly-ing a-lone___ with my head on the phone___
want you to come___ back and car-ry me home___ a-

think-ing of you___ 'til it hurts.___ I know you hurt, too,___ but what
way from these long___ lone-ly nights.___ I'm reach-ing for you.___ Are you

8

AND I LOVE HER

Words and Music by JOHN LENNON
and PAUL McCARTNEY

I know this love of mine___ will nev-er die.___

And I love___ her.___ ___ her.___

AND I LOVE YOU SO

Words and Music by
DON McLEAN

BEIN' GREEN

Words and Music by
JOE RAPOSO

BLUE VELVET

Words and Music by BERNIE WAYNE
and LEE MORRIS

BY THE TIME I GET TO PHOENIX

Words and Music by
JIMMY WEBB

23

CAN'T SMILE WITHOUT YOU

Moderately, with a relaxed beat (♫ = ♪³♪)

Words and Music by CHRIS ARNOLD,
DAVID MARTIN and GEOFF MORROW

CANDLE ON THE WATER

(From Walt Disney Productions' "PETE'S DRAGON")

Words and Music by AL KASHA
and JOEL HIRSCHHORN

Smoothly

I'll be your can-dle on the wa-ter, My love for you will al-ways
I'll be your can-dle on the wa-ter, 'Til ev-'ry wave is warm and

burn. I know you're lost and drift-ing, But the clouds are lift-ing,
bright, My soul is there be-side you, Let this can-dle guide you

don't give up you have some-where to turn.
soon you'll see a gold-en stream of light.

A cold and friend-less tide has found you, don't let the storm-y dark-ness pull you down. I'll paint a ray of hope a-round you, cir-cling in the air light-ed by a prayer. I'll be your can-dle on the wa-ter, this flame in-side of me will

CARELESS WHISPER

Words and Music by GEORGE MICHAEL
and ANDREW RIDGELEY

I feel so un-sure__
Time can nev-er mend__
To - night the mu - sic seems so loud,__ I

___ as I take your hand____ and lead you
the care - less whis - per
wish that we__ could lose this crowd, may - be it's bet - ter this way, if we'd

(THEY LONG TO BE) CLOSE TO YOU

Lyric by HAL DAVID
Music by BURT BACHARACH

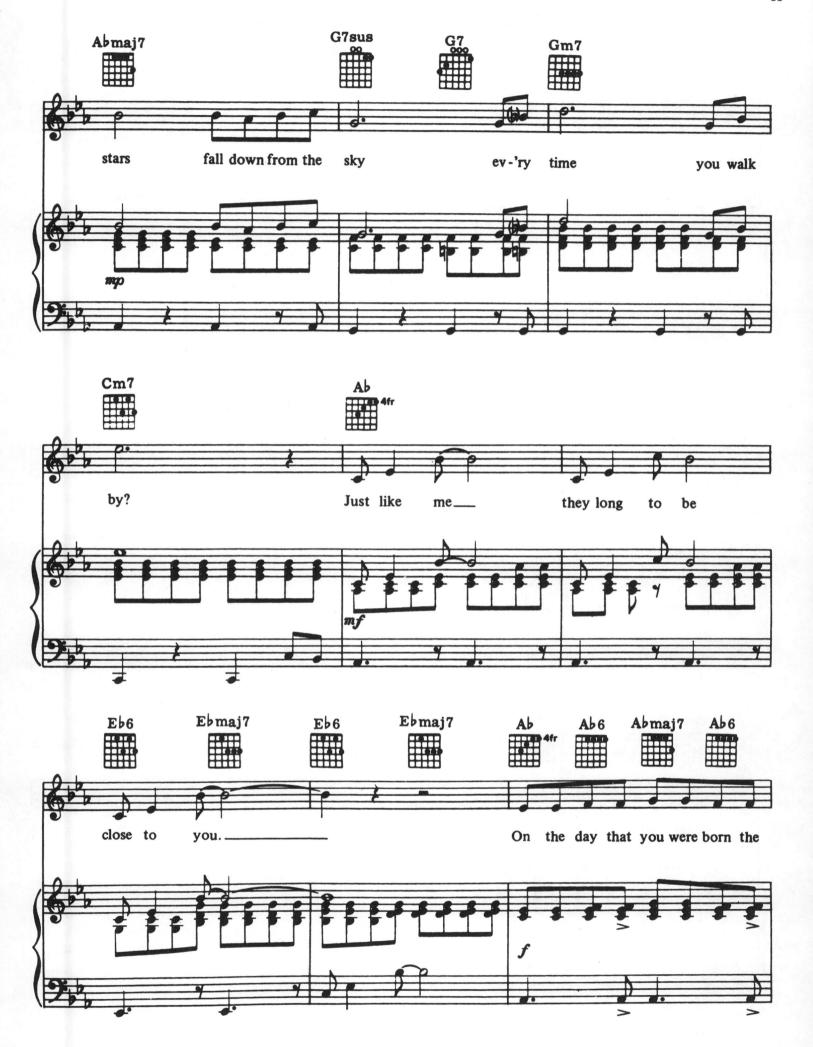

COME IN FROM THE RAIN

Words and Music by MELISSA MANCHESTER
and CAROLE BAYER SAGER

DAYDREAM

Words and Music by JOHN SEBASTIAN

3. *Whistle*
    Whistle
    Whistle
    Whistle
    And you can be sure that if you're feelin' right,
    A daydream will last till long into the night.
    Tomorrow at breakfast you may pick up your ears,
    Or you may be daydreamin' for a thousand years.

DO YOU KNOW THE WAY TO SAN JOSE

Lyric by HAL DAVID
Music by BURT BACHARACH

Do you know the way to San ___ Jo - se?

Can't wait to get back to San ___ Jo - se.

no chord

Repeat and Fade

DON'T LET THE SUN GO DOWN ON ME

Words and Music by ELTON JOHN
and BERNIE TAUPIN

Slow beat

DON'T LET THE SUN CATCH YOU CRYING

Words and Music by GERRARD MARSDEN,
FRED MARSDEN, LES CHADWICK and LES MaGUIRE

Relaxed

DOWNTOWN

Words and Music by TONY HATCH

Medium Rock

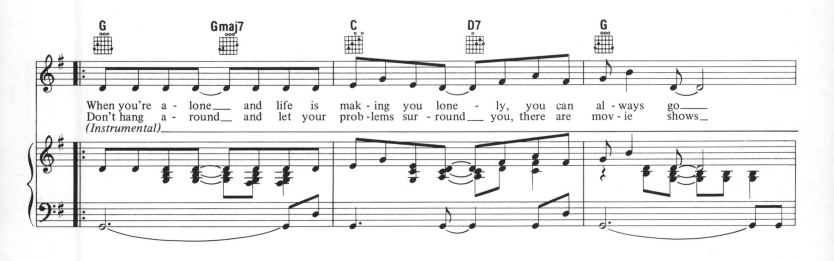

When you're a - lone___ and life is mak - ing you lone - ly, you can al - ways go___
Don't hang a - round___ and let your prob - lems sur - round___ you, there are mov - ie shows___
*(Instrumental)*___

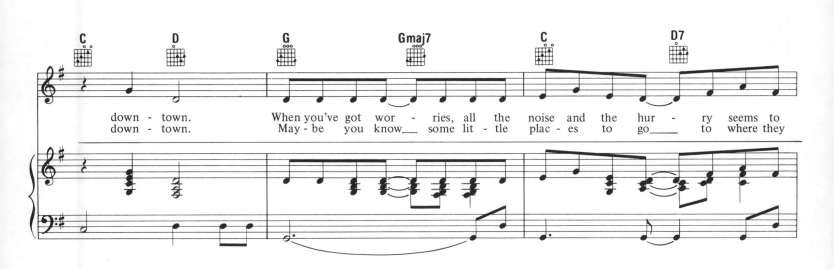

down - town. When you've got wor - ries, all the noise and the hur - ry seems to
down - town. May - be you know___ some lit - tle plac - es to go___ to where they

MCA music publishing

DUST IN THE WIND

Moderate Folk style

Words and Music by
KERRY LIVGREN

close my eyes
Same old hang
Don't

on - ly for a mo - ment, and the mo - ment's gone.
Just a drop of wa - ter in an end - less sea.
Noth - ing lasts for - ev - er but the earth and sky.
It

EVERY BREATH YOU TAKE

Words and Music by
STING

EYE IN THE SKY

Word and Music by ALAN PARSONS
and ERIC WOOLFSON

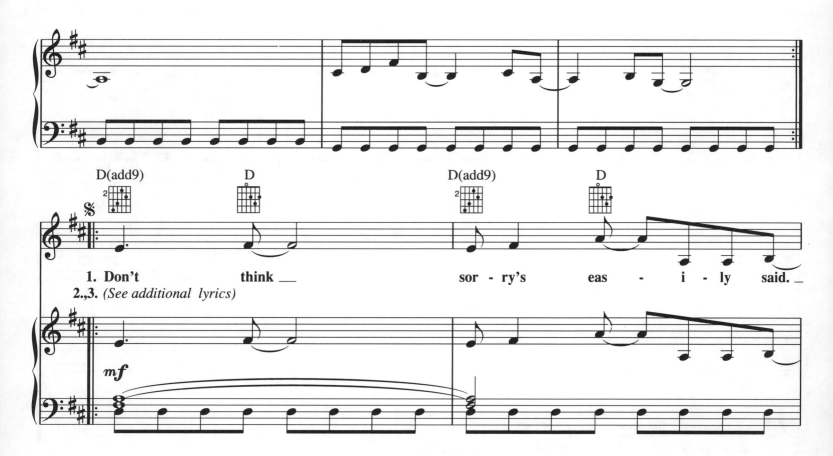

1. **Don't** think _____ **sor - ry's eas - i - ly said.**
2.,3. *(See additional lyrics)*

part of me knows_ what you're think - ing.

I am the

eye in the sky, ___ look - ing at you; ___

___ I can read_ your mind. _ I am the mak - er of rules _

I am the

(Begin instrumental solo, ad lib.)

Repeat ad lib. and Fade

Additional Lyrics

2. Don't say words you're gonna regret.
   Don't let the fire rush to your head.
   I've heard the accusation before,
   And I ain't gonna take any more,
   Believe me.
   The sun in your eyes
   Made some of the lies worth believing.
   (To Chorus:)

3. Don't leave false illusions behind.
   Don't cry 'cause I ain't changing my mind.
   So find another fool like before,
   'Cause I ain't gonna live anymore believing
   Some of the lies, while all of the signs are deceiving.
   (To Chorus:)

FOR ALL WE KNOW
(From The Motion Picture "LOVERS AND OTHER STRANGERS")

Words by ROBB WILSON and JAMES GRIFFIN
Music by FRED KARLIN

Moderato, with a light beat

GOIN' OUT OF MY HEAD

Words and Music by TEDDY RANDAZZO
and BOBBY WEINSTEIN

GREEN GREEN GRASS OF HOME

Words and Music by
CURLY PUTMAN

Moderately Slow

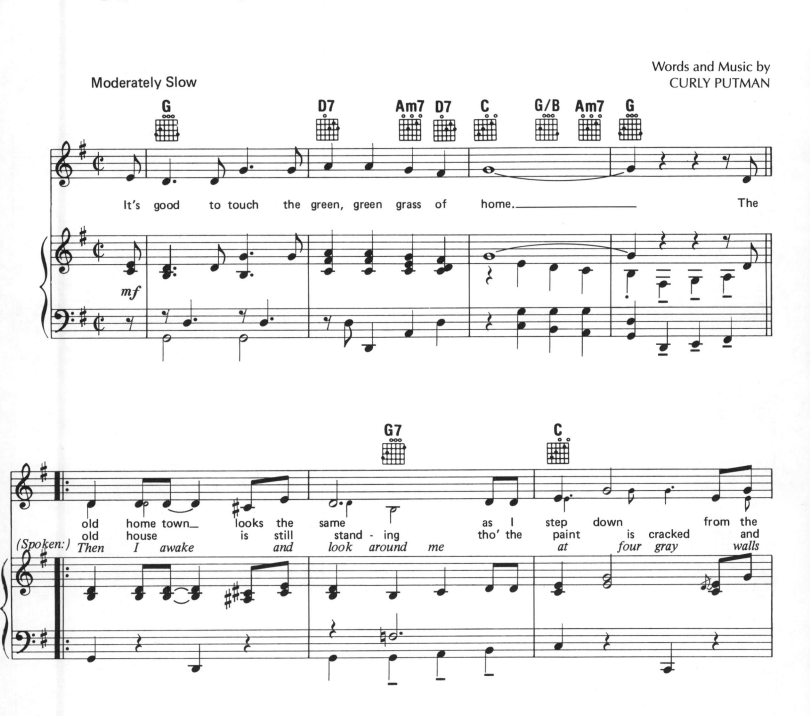

It's good to touch the green, green grass of home. _____ The

old home town____ looks the same as I step down from the
(Spoken:) Then I awake and look around me at four gray walls

train,_____ and there to meet me is my ma - ma____ and
dry,_____ and there's that old oak tree that I used____ to
that surround me and I realize that I was only dreaming.

HELLO AGAIN
(From the motion picture THE JAZZ SINGER)

Words by NEIL DIAMOND
Music by NEIL DIAMOND and ALAN LINDGREN

Moderately slow

Hel - lo a- gain, hel - lo. Just called to say 'hel - lo'. I could - n't sleep at all to-night. And I know it's late, but I

HERE COMES THAT RAINY DAY FEELING AGAIN

Words and Music by TONY MACAULAY,
ROGER COOK and ROGER GREENAWAY

88

HEY JUDE

Words and Music by JOHN LENNON
and PAUL McCARTNEY

HOW AM I SUPPOSED TO LIVE WITHOUT YOU

Words and Music by MICHAEL BOLTON
and DOUG JAMES

I could hard-ly be - lieve____ it when I
I'm too proud for cry - ing, did - n't

heard the news__ to - day.__ I had to come__ and get it straight__ from you.
come here to break down.__ It's just a dream of mine__ is com - in' to__ an end.__

They said you are leav - in' some-one's
And how can I blame__ you when I

HOW DEEP IS YOUR LOVE

Words and Music by BARRY GIBB,
MAURICE GIBB and ROBIN GIBB

Moderately

I know your eyes in the morn - ing sun.____ I feel you touch
I be - lieve in you.____ You know the door.

____ me in the pour - ing rain.____ And the mo - ment that you wan - der far__
____ to my ver - y soul.____ You're the light ____ in my deep - est, dark

I DREAMED A DREAM

(From "LES MISERABLES")

Lyrics by HERBERT KRETZMER
Original text by ALAIN BOUBLIL and JEAN-MARC NATEL
Music by CLAUDE-MICHEL SCHÖNBERG

I JUST FALL IN LOVE AGAIN

Words and Music by
LARRY HERBSTRITT, STEPHEN H. DORFF,
GLORIA SKLEROV and HARRY LLOYD

I.O.U.

Words and Music by AUSTIN ROBERTS
and KERRY CHATER

Moderately Slow Ballad

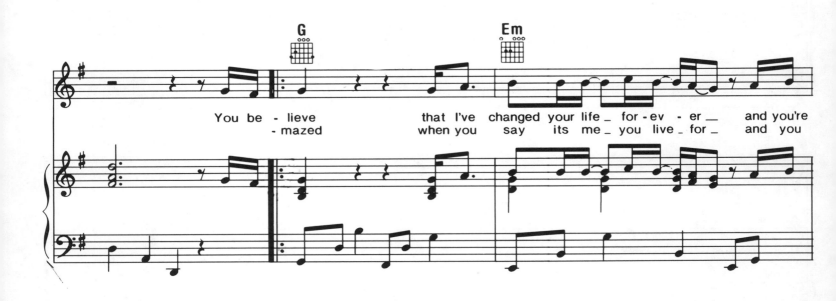

You be - lieve that I've changed your life _ for - ev - er _ and you're
- mazed when you say its me _ you live _ for _ and you

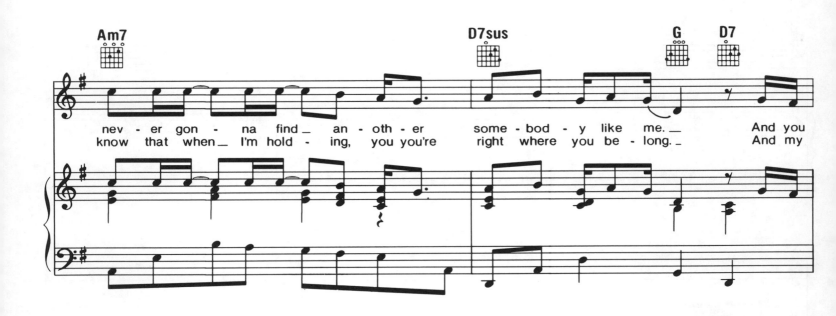

nev - er gon - na find _ an - oth - er some - bod - y like me. _ And you
know that when _ I'm hold - ing, you you're right where you be - long. _ And my

112

I WOULDN'T HAVE MISSED IT FOR THE WORLD

Words and Music by KYE FLEMING,
DENNIS MORGAN and CHARLES QUILLEN

114

C   Am7   D7   B7/D#

one mem - o - ry, ___ 'cause you mean ___ too much to me. ___

Em   D7   Am7

E - ven though ___ I lost ___ you, girl, ___

D7sus   1 D7   2,3 D7   D.S. twice and Fade

I would-n't have missed ___ it for ___ the world. ___ it for ___ the world. ___

Verse 2.
They say that all good things must end.
Love comes and goes just like the wind.
You've got your dreams to follow,
But if I had the chance tomorrow,
You know I'd do it all again.
(To Chorus)

I WRITE THE SONGS

Words and Music by
BRUCE JOHNSTON

I'LL NEVER FALL IN LOVE AGAIN

Lyric by HAL DAVID
Music by BURT BACHARACH

I'M EASY

Words and Music by KEITH CARRADINE

MCA music publishing

IMAGINE

Words and Music by
JOHN LENNON

Im-ag-ine there's no hea-ven.

It's eas-y if you try.

No hell be-low us,

IT WAS A VERY GOOD YEAR

Words and Music by
ERVIN DRAKE

135

IT NEVER RAINS
(IN SOUTHERN CALIFORNIA)

Words and Music by RAY WIGGINS
and TIM CHRISTIAN

Moderately slow
no chord

mp

Gm7

It nev-er rains _ in south-ern Cal - i - for - nia. I'll see you when _ I get there.

Gm7/C

I hav-en't seen your face _ in a year,
May-be I'll take a flight _ out to-night,
We have so much to talk _ a-bout,
Now since I've been here at _ your place,

I can't wait _ till I _ get there. _
and you could pick me up _ a-bout eight.
a lot of catch-ing up _ to do.
let's take a _ week's trip _ for two. _

Just a kiss,__ and squeeze, __ and hug, __ and girl, ___ you know __ the rest, as they tell __ me:
I don't know __ what air - line girl, __ but I know we won't __ be late, 'cause they tell __ me:
I'll bring __ the dia - mond girl, __ be - cause I'm so in - to you, 'cause they tell __ me:
We don't have __ to go ___ too far, __ just as long as I'm __ with you, 'cause they tell me:

Cm7/F

It nev-er rains __ in south-ern Cal - i - for - nia. And they tell __ me:

Gm7/C

[1]

It nev-er rains __ in south - ern Cal - i - for - nia.

[2]

Fm11   Gm11   Abmaj7   Gm7   Cm7

- nia.

Now, I can't sleep at night,__ with -
Can we just be a - lone, __ with -

KOKOMO

Words and Music by MIKE LOVE, TERRY MELCHER,
JOHN PHILLIPS, and SCOTT McKENZIE

Moderately bright

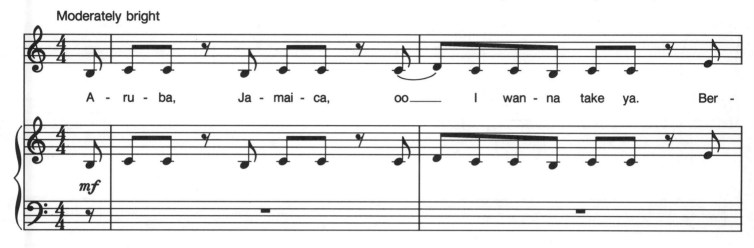

A - ru - ba, Ja - mai - ca, oo___ I wan - na take ya. Ber -

mu - da, Ba - ha - ma, come___ on, pret - ty ma - ma. Key Lar - go, Mon - te - go, Ba -

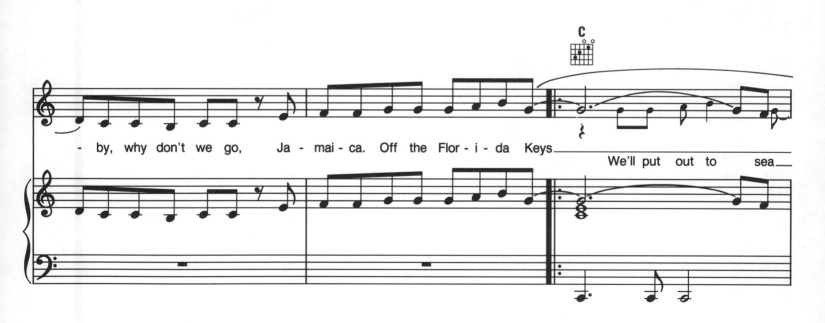

- by, why don't we go, Ja - mai - ca. Off the Flor - i - da Keys___
We'll put out to sea___

144

JUST ONCE

Words by CYNTHIA WEIL
Music by BARRY MANN

I did my best, _____ but I
I gave my all, _____ but I

guess my best _ was-n't good _ e-nough _ 'cause here we are _ back _ where we were _ be-fore,
think my all _ may have been _ too much _ 'cause Lord knows, we're _ not _ get-ting an - y-where, _

Seems noth-ing ev - er chang - es, we're
It seems we're al - ways blow - in' what-

THE LAST TIME I FELT LIKE THIS
(From "SAME TIME, NEXT YEAR")

Words by ALAN BERGMAN
and MARILYN BERGMAN
Music by MARVIN HAMLISCH

LET IT BE ME
(JE T'APPARTIENS)

English Words by MANN CURTIS
French Words by PIERRE DELANOE
Music by GILBERT BECAUD

I bless the day I found you, I want to stay a - round you,
If, for each bit of glad - ness, Some - one must taste of sad - ness,

And so I beg you, let it be me. Don't take this
I'll bear the sor - row, let it be me. No mat - ter

heav - en from one, If you must cling to some - one, Now and for - ev - er,
what the price is, I'll make the sac - ri - fic - es, Through each to - mor - row,

Lookin' For Love

Words and Music by WANDA MALLETTE,
PATTI RYAN and BOB MORRISON

LOST IN YOUR EYES

Words and Music by
DEBORAH GIBSON

LOVE TAKES TIME

Words and Music by MARIAH CAREY
and BEN MARGULIES

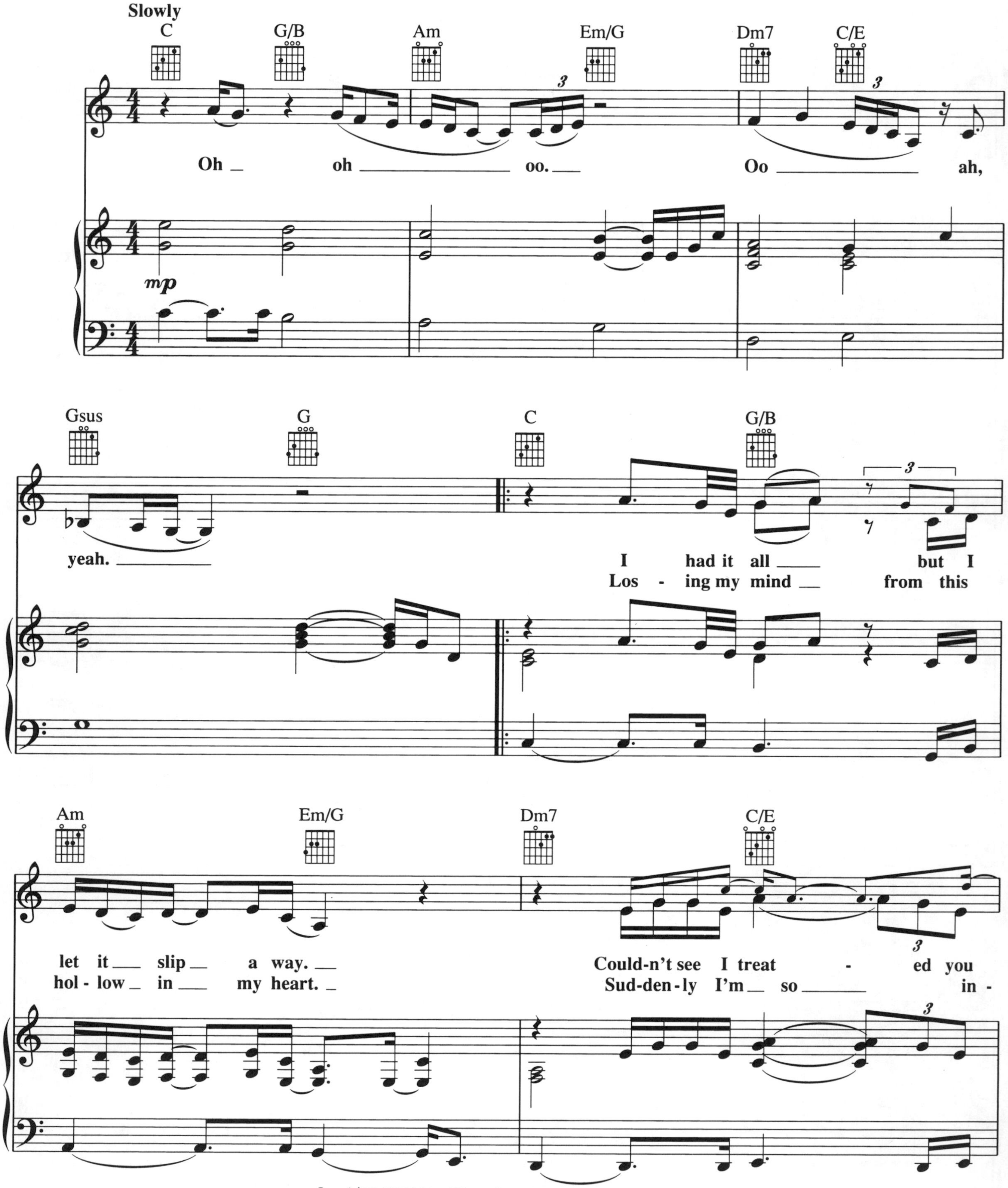

Slowly
C
G/B
Am
Em/G
Dm7
C/E
Oh _ oh _ oo. _ Oo _ ah,
mp
Gsus
G
C
G/B
yeah. _
I had it all _ but I
Los - ing my mind _ from this
Am
Em/G
Dm7
C/E
let it _ slip _ a way. _
hol - low _ in _ my heart. _
Could-n't see I treat - ed you
Sud-den-ly I'm _ so _ in -

MAKE THE WORLD GO AWAY

By HANK COCHRAN

MANDY

Words and Music by
SCOTT ENGLISH and RICHARD KERR

178

MIDNIGHT TRAIN TO GEORGIA

Words and Music by
JIM WEATHERLY

184

MY FAVORITE THINGS
(From "THE SOUND OF MUSIC")

Lyrics by OSCAR HAMMERSTEIN II
Music by RICHARD RODGERS

187

ONE VOICE

Words and Music by
BARRY MANILOW

Slowly, with much feeling

Just One Voice, _____ Sing - ing in the dark - ness, _____

_____ All it takes is One Voice, _____ Sing - ing so they

hear what's on your mind, And when you look a - round you'll find There's more than

one   will   sing! _____

Instrumental Solo

PIANO MAN

Words and Music by
BILLY JOEL

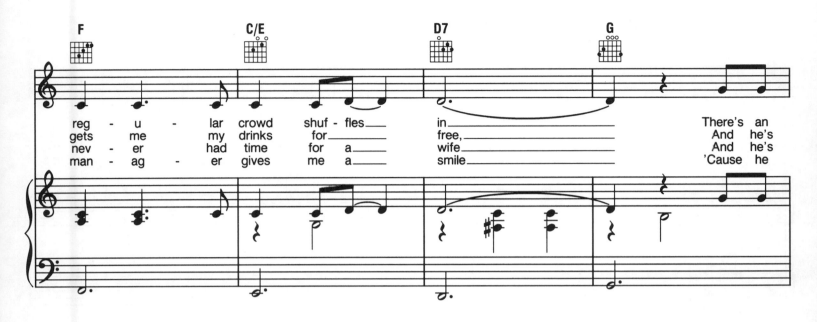

reg - u - lar crowd shuf - fles___ in___ There's an
gets me my drinks for___ free,___ And he's
nev - er had time for a___ wife___ And he's
man - ag - er gives me a___ smile___ 'Cause he

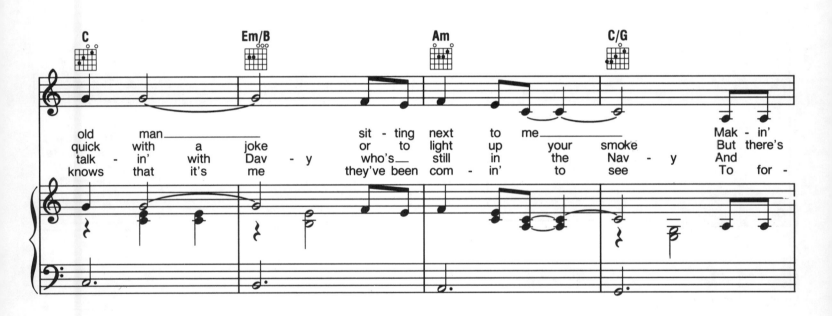

old man___ sit - ting next to me___ Mak - in'
quick with a joke or to light up your smoke But there's
talk - in' with Dav - y who's still in the Nav - y And
knows that it's me they've been com - in' to see To for -

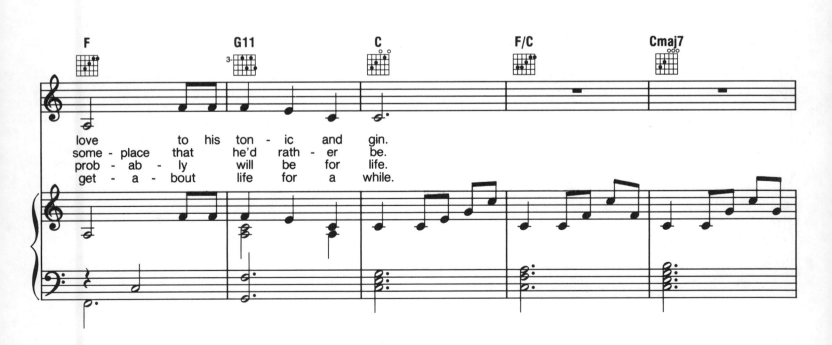

love to his ton - ic and gin.
some - place that he'd rath - er be.
prob - ab - ly will be for life.
get - a - bout life for a while.

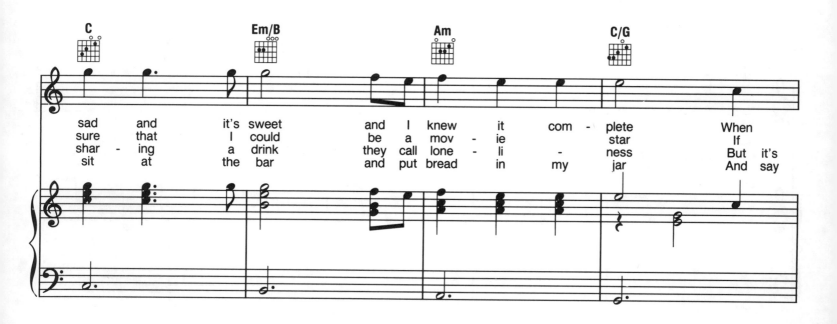

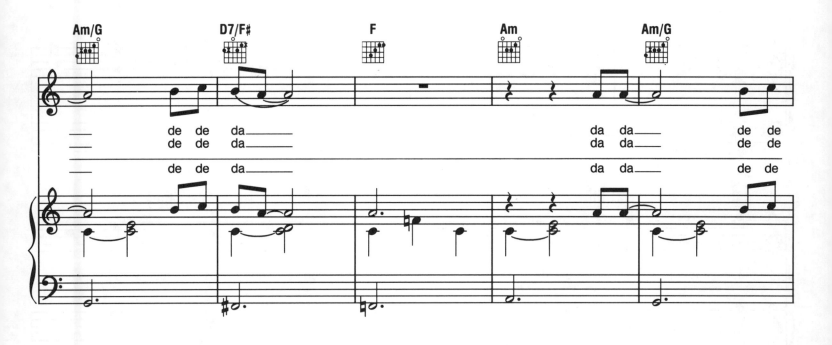

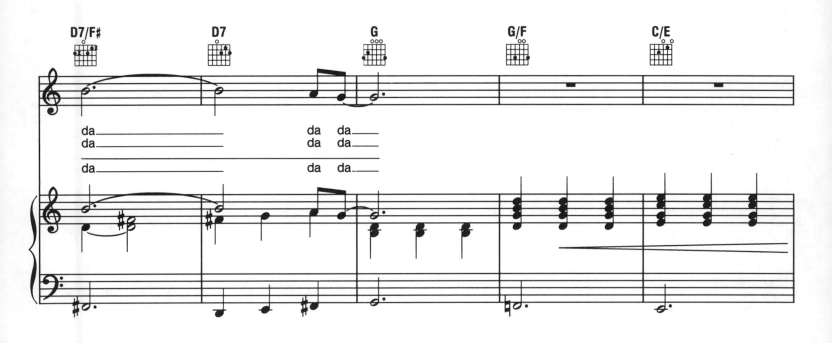

PLEASE COME TO BOSTON

Words and Music by DAVE LOGGINS

1. Please come to Bos-ton for the spring-time. I'm
2. Please come to Den-ver with the snow-fall. We'll

stay-ing here with some friends and they've got lots of room.
move up in-to the moun-tains so far that we can't be found and

You can sell your paint-ings on the side-walk, by a ca-fé where I
throw 'I love you' ech-o's down the can-yons. And then lie a-wake at

ADDITIONAL LYRICS

Verse 3.
    Please come to L.A. to live forever
    A California life alone is just too hard to build
    I live in a house that looks out over the ocean
    And there's some stars that fell from the sky
    Living up on the hill
    Please come to L.A., she just said no,
    Boy, won't you come home to me.
Repeat Chorus

QUIET NIGHTS OF QUIET STARS
(CORCOVADO)

Original Words and Music by
ANTONIO CARLOS JOBIM
English Words by
GENE LEES

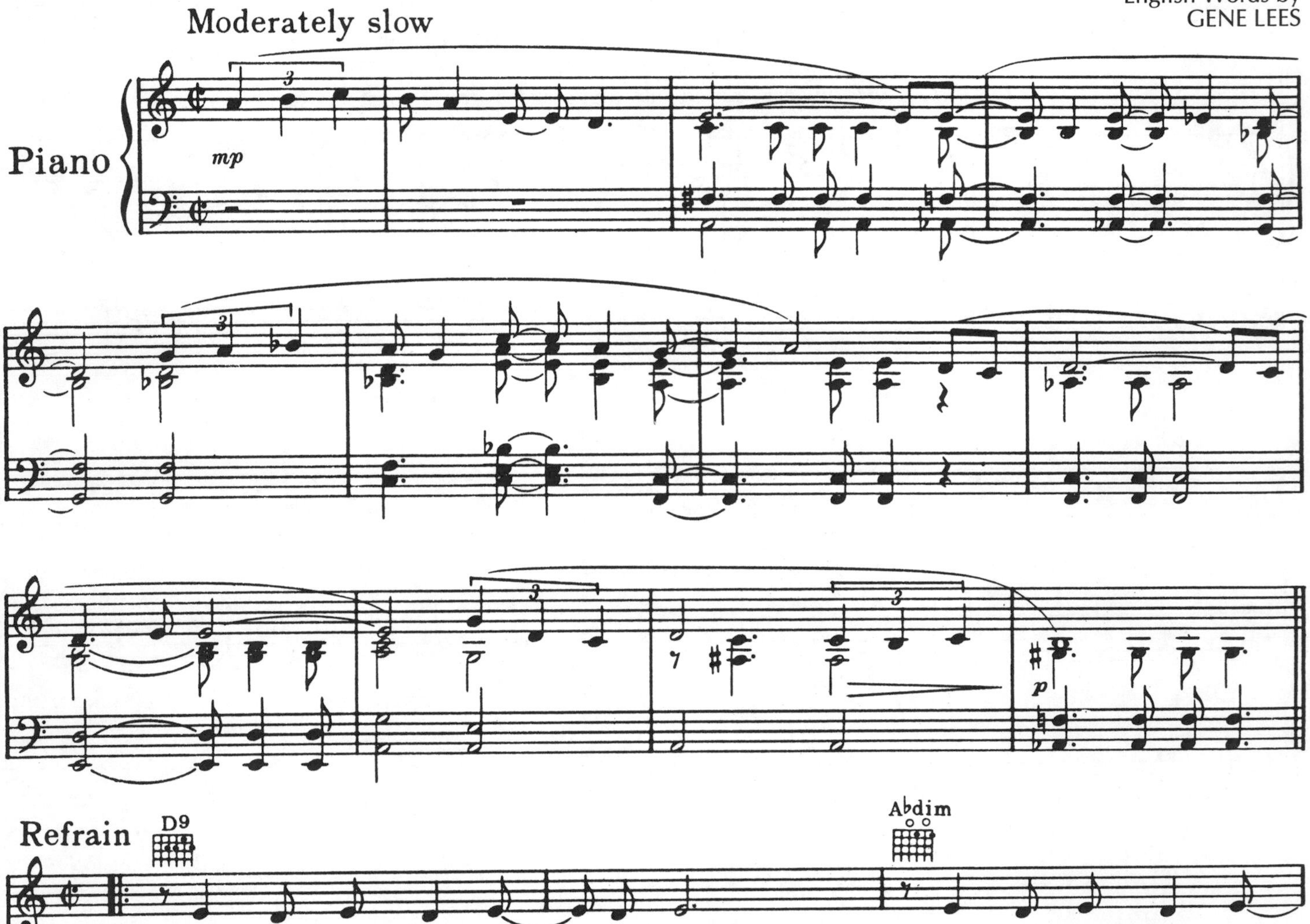

Refrain

QUI - ET NIGHTS OF QUI - ET STARS, qui - et chords from my gui - tar float - ing on the si ___ lence that ___ sur - rounds ___

MCA music publishing

THE RAINBOW CONNECTION

By PAUL WILLIAMS and
KENNETH L. ASCHER

Why are there so man-y songs a - bout rain - bows, and
Who said that ev - 'ry wish would be heard and an - swered when

what's on the oth - er side? _____
wished on the morn - ing star? _____

Rain - bows are vis - ions, ___ but on - ly il - lu - sions, And
Some - bod - y thought of that, and some - one be - lieved it;

SAILING

Words and Music by
CHRISTOPHER CROSS

Sail - ing takes me a - way _ to where _ i've al - ways heard it _ could be. _ Just a dream _ and the wind _ to car - ry me, and soon I will _ be free. _

SHE'S LIKE THE WIND

Music and Lyrics by PATRICK SWAYZE
and STACY WIDELITZ

SHE BELIEVES IN ME

Slowly with movement

Words & Music by STEVE GIBB

223

SING

Words and Music by
JOE RAPOSO

SOMETHING

Words and Music by
GEORGE HARRISON

Some-thing in___ the way___ she moves,___
Some-where in___ her smile___ she knows,___
Some-thing in___ the way___ she knows,___

at-tracts___ me like___ no oth-er lov___-er.
that I___ don't need___ no oth-er lov___-er.
and all___ I have___ to do is think___ of her.

Some-thing in___ the way___ she woos___ me.___
Some-thing in___ her style___ that shows___ me.___
Some-thing in___ the things___ she shows___ me.___

I don't want to leave___ her now,___ you

SMOKY MOUNTAIN RAIN

Words and Music by KYE FLEMING
and DENNIS MORGAN

SONG SUNG BLUE

Words and Music by
NEIL DIAMOND

239

Fun-ny thing__ but you can sing ___ it with a cry in your voice, ___ And be-fore you know it start to feel-in' good ___ you sim-ply got no choice. ___

D.S. al Coda

CODA

SUNRISE, SUNSET
(From "FIDDLER ON THE ROOF")

Words by SHELDON HARNICK
Music by JERRY BOCK

Moderately Slow Waltz Tempo
(soulful and wistful)

UNEXPECTED SONG
(From "SONG & DANCE")

Music by Andrew Lloyd Webber
Lyrics by Don Black

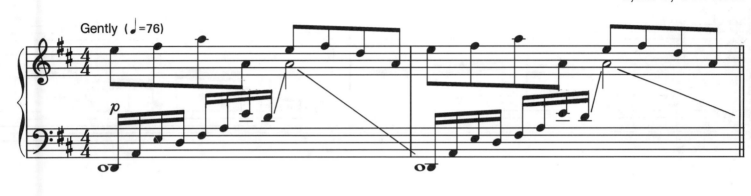

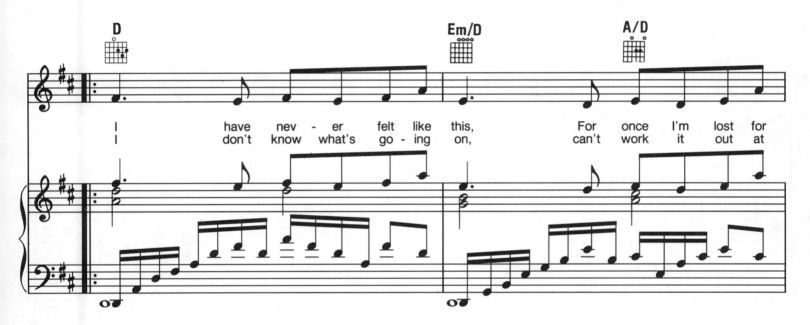

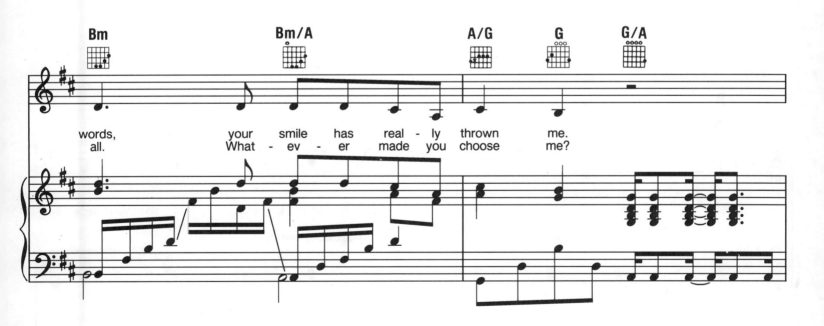

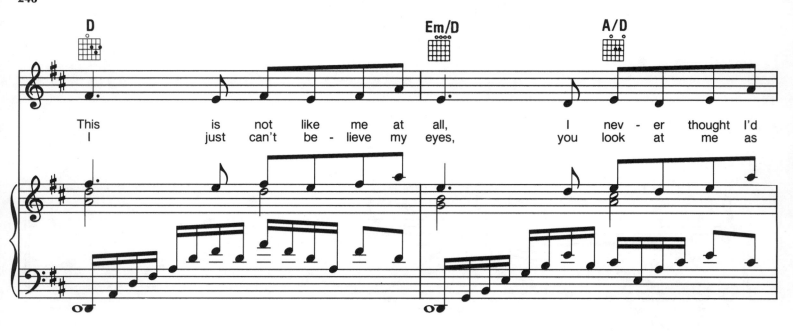

This is not like me at all, I nev - er thought I'd
I just can't be - lieve my eyes, you look at me as

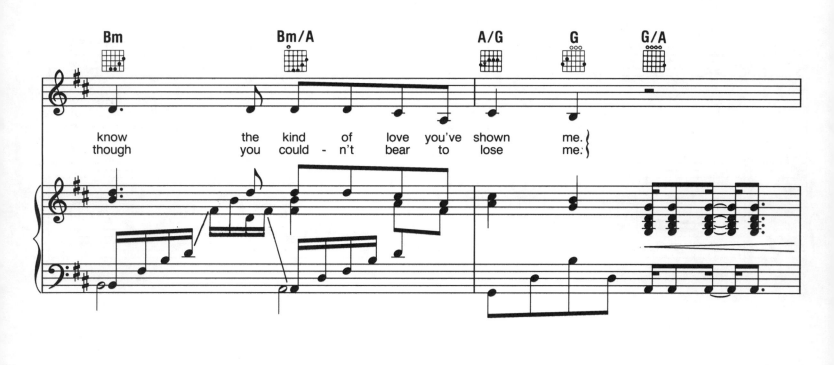

know the kind of love you've shown me.
though you could - n't bear to lose me.

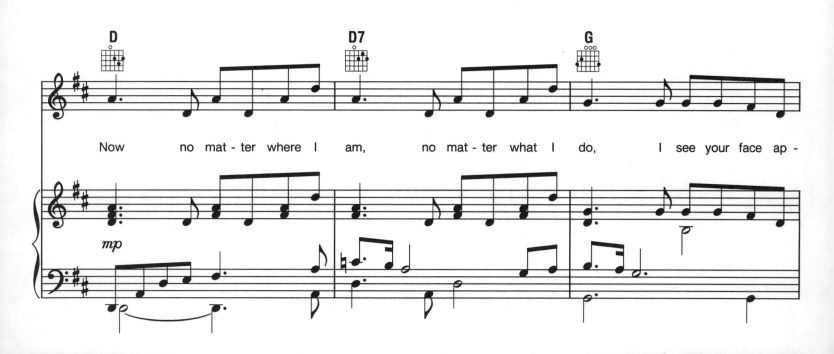

Now no mat - ter where I am, no mat - ter what I do, I see your face ap -

thrown me. This is not like me at all, I nev-er thought I'd

know the kind of love you've shown me. Now no mat-ter where I

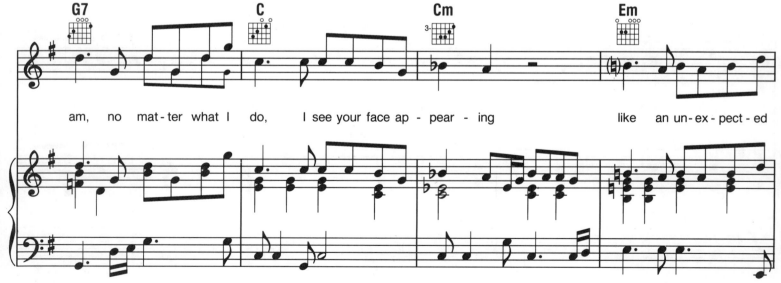

am, no mat-ter what I do, I see your face ap-pear-ing like an un-ex-pect-ed

THIS GUY'S IN LOVE WITH YOU

Lyric by HAL DAVID
Music by BURT BACHARACH

THIS ONE'S FOR YOU

Words by MARTY PANZER
Music by BARRY MANILOW

To Coda

say that noth - ing's been the same since we've been a - part.
say the things I should have said, things that you should know.

This one's for all the love we once knew,

Like ev - ery - thing else I have, This One's For You, oh.

D.S. to 2nd ending al Coda

TO ALL THE GIRLS I'VE LOVED BEFORE

Lyric by HAL DAVID
Music by ALBERT HAMMOND

Moderately slow, with expression

To all the girls I've loved be-fore,
once car-essed,
shared my life,

who trav-eled in and
and may I say I've
who now are some-one

out my door;
held the best;
els-e's wife;

I'm glad they came a-long,
for help-ing me to grow,
I'm glad they came a-long,

I ded-i-cate this
I owe a lot, I
I ded-i-cate this

259

UNCHAINED MELODY

Words by HY ZARET
Music by ALEX NORTH

264

265

VINCENT
(STARRY, STARRY NIGHT)

Words and Music by
DON McLEAN

VISION OF LOVE

Words and Music by MARIAH CAREY
and BEN MARGULIES

WHAT A WONDERFUL WORLD

Words and Music by GEORGE DAVID WEISS
and BOB THIELE

WHAT THE WORLD NEEDS NOW
IS LOVE

Lyric by HAL DAVID
Music by BURT BACHARACH

282

WHAT'S FOREVER FOR

Words and Music by
RAFE VANHOY

Moderately Slow

I've been look-ing at peo - ple and how they change with the times;

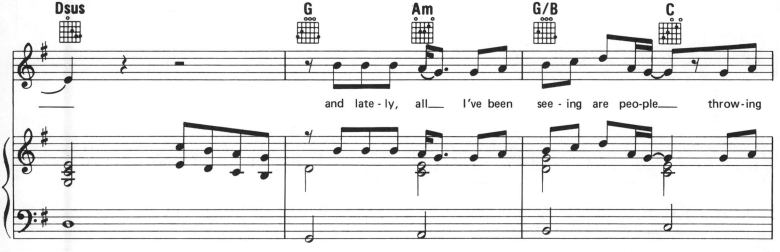

and late-ly, all I've been see-ing are peo-ple throw-ing

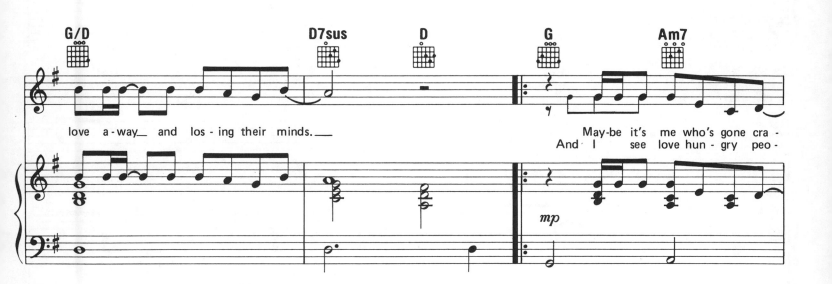

love a-way and los-ing their minds.

May-be it's me who's gone cra-
And I see love hun-gry peo-

WOMAN

Words and Music by
JOHN LENNON

YOU DECORATED MY LIFE

Words and Music by DEBBIE HUPP
and BOB MORRISON

All my life was a pa - per once plain, pure and white;
rhyme with no rea - son in an un - fin - ished song;

Till you moved with your pen chang - in' moods now and then till the
There was no har - mo - ny life meant noth - in' to me, un - til

bal - ance was right. Then you add - ed some mu - sic,
you came a - long. And you brought out the col - ors,

290

You Give Good Love

Words and Music by
LAFORREST "LA LA" COPE

MCA music publishing

YOUR SONG

Words and Music by ELTON JOHN
and TAUPIN

that I put down in words, how won-der-ful life is while

you're in the world.

you're in the world.